EXPLORERS DISCOVERING THE WORLD

THE EXPLORATION OF AFRICA

Tim Cooke

Gareth Stevens
Publishing

Please visit our website, www.garethstevens.com. For a free color catalog of all our high-quality books, call toll-free 1-800-542-2595 or fax 1-877-542-2596.

Library of Congress Cataloging-in-Publication Data

Cooke, Tim, 1961-
 The exploration of Africa / Tim Cooke.
    p. cm. — (Explorers discovering the world)
 Includes index.
ISBN 978-1-4339-8612-3 (pbk.)
ISBN 978-1-4339-8613-0 (6-pack)
ISBN 978-1-4339-8611-6 (library binding)
1. Africa--Discovery and exploration--European--Juvenile literature. 2. Explorers—Africa—Biography—Juvenile literature. 3. Explorers—Europe—Biography—Juvenile literature. 4. Europeans—Africa—History—Juvenile literature. I. Title. II. Series: Explorers discovering the world.
 DT3.C67 2013
 916.04—dc23

                                        2012024372

Published in 2013 by
Gareth Stevens Publishing
111 East 14th Street, Suite 349
New York, NY 10003

© 2013 Brown Bear Books Ltd

For Brown Bear Books Ltd:
Editorial Director: Lindsey Lowe
Managing Editor: Tim Cooke
Children's Publisher: Anne O'Daly
Art Director: Jeni Child
Designer: Lynne Lennon
Picture Manager: Sophie Mortimer

Picture Credits
Front Cover: Shutterstock: main: Thinkstock; inset: Photos.com

Alamy: Mary Evans Picture Library 29; **Clipart.com:** 13; **Library of Congress:** 31, 42; **Mary Evans Picture Library:** 34; **Public Domain:** 19, 25, 39, Civitates Orbis Terrarum/Braun and Hoggenberg 14–15, Dudley Essex 35, Didier Tais 45, Dorothy Voorhees 26; **Shutterstock:** 37, Antonio Abrignani 20, Abraham Badenhorst 10, James Michael Dorsey 21, Maej Hudovernik 44–45, Pecold 32, Graeme Shannon 33, Dietmar Temps 41; **Thinkstock:** Ablestock 5t, Ingram Publishing 5b, Goodshoot 17, Hemera 18, 23, 30, istockphoto 8, 9, 11, 15, 27, 28, 36, Photos.com 6, 7, 12, 16, 38, 40, 43; **Topfoto:** The Granger Collection 22, 24.

Brown Bear Books has made every attempt to contact copyright holders. If anyone has any information, please contact smortimer@windmillbooks.co.uk.

Manufactured in the United States of America
1 2 3 4 5 6 7 8 9 12 11 10

CPSIA compliance information: Batch #CW13GS: For further information contact Gareth Stevens, New York, New York at 1-800-542-2595.

CONTENTS

INTRODUCTION

In the mid-19th century, Africa was still little known to Europeans, who called it "the dark continent." The daunting terrain included deserts, jungles, mountains, and rivers with dangerous rapids. The climate encouraged disease, which killed dozens of explorers. There was also danger from hostile peoples.

But European knowledge of Africa was slowly growing. By exploring great rivers such as the Niger and the Nile, travelers were putting together an understanding of the heart of the continent.

Colonial Pressure

From the early 1800s, European countries began to acquire territory in Africa. French explorers crossed the Sahara and claimed virtually the whole of North Africa. The British led the way in west Africa and in the south and east. The Belgian king set up a colony in central Africa in the 1880s. By the end of the century, the whole continent had been claimed by one or other of the European powers in the "scramble for Africa."

The lack of accurate detail on this old map sums up the lack of knowledge the Europeans had about what lay beyond the coasts of Africa.

Many European explorers had friendly relations with native Africans, but European governments often treated Africa as though no one lived there.

1418–1460

HENRY THE NAVIGATOR

Prester John was said to be a powerful Christian king in Africa; Henry hoped his explorers would learn news of the legendary kingdom.

In the early 15th century, the Portuguese started to explore the west coast of Africa. The man who led the way was a royal prince, Henry. A deeply religious man, Henry devoted his life to exploration. He earned the nickname "Henry the Navigator."

Henry was not the first Portuguese to want to find out what lay across the sea. His father, King John I, had led an expedition to an Arab port in North Africa in 1415.

Sailing South

Henry commissioned his first expedition in 1418. It got as far south as the island of Porto Santo in the Madeiras, off the coast of present-day Morocco. During the 1420s, Henry sent more expeditions. They gradually inched south along the African coast as far as Cape Bojador, now in the Western Sahara, just south of the Canary Islands.

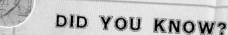
Prince Henry wanted to explore Africa partly to find a sea route to India by sailing around the southern tip of the continent. That would open rich trade routes.

PRESTER JOHN

One of the attractions of Africa for Prince Henry was the hope of making contact with Prester John. From the 11th century, rumors swept Europe that Prester John ruled a Christian kingdom somewhere in Africa. European rulers thought he would be a useful ally against the Muslim kingdoms of the Middle East. Henry hoped to find Prester John's legendary kingdom, which he thought was in Abyssinia (now Ethiopia in eastern Africa).

DID YOU KNOW?

Henry founded a school of navigation. He also oversaw the improvement of ships and navigational tools like the quadrant.

The rocky coast of Madeira was a common staging post for Portuguese sailors heading down the coast of Africa or returning home.

Henry's explorers reached the Senegal River and then sailed around Cape Verde, the westernmost point of Africa. They brought home gold dust and black-skinned Africans.

Spirit of Adventure

Henry's explorers were squires, young nobles whose taste for adventure was more important than their learning. They included João Fernandes, who was stuck ashore for months. When he was rescued, he told stories about the Berber and Azenegue people he had met.

In 1455, a Venetian merchant, Alvise da Cadamosto, persuaded Henry that the exploration of Africa could offer economic possibilities. Henry commissioned Cadamosto to set up trading connections with local people along the African coast.

More Progress

Cadamosto explored the Senegal River, reaching 60 miles (100 km) inland. He sailed up the Gambia River, recording everything he saw. By the time Henry died in 1460, he was convinced that his sailors would soon find a route around Africa to India.

DID YOU KNOW?

The Portuguese developed a new ship to explore the African coast; the caravel was larger and stronger than previous ships.

"DARK CONTINENT"

For European explorers, much of Africa was unknown until the 15th century. They only knew the northern coast; they did not know what, if anything, lay south of the vast Sahara Desert. In fact, Arab and Berber traders had long before crossed the Sahara looking for gold. Arab sailors had traveled down the east coast as far as the island of Zanzibar. Africa was nothing like as unknown as Europeans thought.

Henry's school of navigation helped sailors, shipbuilders, merchants, and mapmakers study improved ways of navigation.

1487–1488

BARTOLOMEU DIAS

This statue of Dias stands in Cape Town, South Africa, near where the Portuguese rounded the southern tip of the continent.

Dias was a Portuguese nobleman who accidentally discovered what Portuguese sailors had been seeking for decades: the southern tip of Africa. But although that had been Henry the Navigator's ambition, the discovery was of far less interest to the Portuguese rulers in the 1480s.

DID YOU KNOW?

Navigators used the astrolabe to take sightings of the stars. It was easier to use on a moving ship than the quadrant.

Dias called the tip of Africa the "Cape of Storms"; King John II of Portugal later renamed it the "Cape of Good Hope" because it offered a route to the Indies.

Dias's ships—two caravels and a supply ship—sailed down the west coast of Africa in 1487. He probably sailed around west Africa and then followed the coastline as far as Namibia.

Lucky Storm

A massive storm carried Dias's ships out to sea. When the men next made land, they were at the Cape of Good Hope. The coast was curving northeast. At last, the tip of Africa had been reached.

Dias sailed back to Lisbon, arriving in December 1488. But it would be seven years before a new expedition was commissioned to follow up on his discovery.

RULE OF THE SUN

Navigators charted their way by the stars. As they neared the equator, however, the Portuguese found that familiar stars sank beneath the horizon. In 1484, Portuguese mathematicians worked out a way to navigate by plotting the path of the sun. The highest altitude of the sun indicated the ship's current latitude.

1497–1498

VASCO DA GAMA

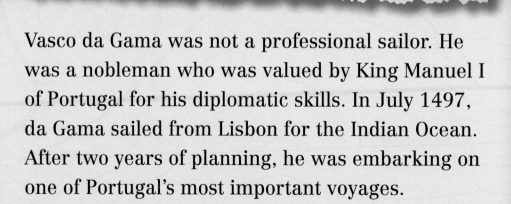

Da Gama's fleet had two large naos and a caravel; there was also a storeship, which was left on the African coast.

Vasco da Gama was not a professional sailor. He was a nobleman who was valued by King Manuel I of Portugal for his diplomatic skills. In July 1497, da Gama sailed from Lisbon for the Indian Ocean. After two years of planning, he was embarking on one of Portugal's most important voyages.

Da Gama took two *naos* (large ships), a caravel, and a storeship. He sailed to the Cape Verde Islands and then out into the Atlantic. After a wrong turn, he eventually sailed around the Cape of Good Hope.

Seeking Help

Da Gama headed up the east coast of Africa until he reached Mozambique Town. The town was the center for Arabian trade across the Indian Ocean. Da Gama tried to find guides for his voyage, but the Muslim ruler of Mozambique refused to give any help.

CARRACK

Da Gama's route to India opened the Indian Ocean to Portuguese carracks. The carrack was the largest merchant ship of the time. The vessel could carry more than 600 tons (545 t) of cargo, was sturdy in rough seas, and could be armed. The carracks had either three or four masts; they had square or triangular (lateen) sails. If necessary, Portuguese carracks could fight off Muslim vessels in the Indian Ocean.

The sea route to India that da Gama found was the first chance Europeans had to challenge Muslim control of overland trade with Asia.

DID YOU KNOW?

When da Gama reached the Cape, he had been at sea for 13 weeks, the longest sea voyage yet made by Europeans.

Da Gama kidnapped sailors, but they refused to help him. In Mombasa, Kenya, he received another hostile welcome. It seemed that no Muslim ruler would help Christian Europeans.

Change of Luck

Da Gama's luck changed at the next port, Malindi. Not only did the sultan welcome him, but the greatest navigator of the Indian Ocean, Ibn Madjid, was in port. He had even written down details of the best routes across the ocean.

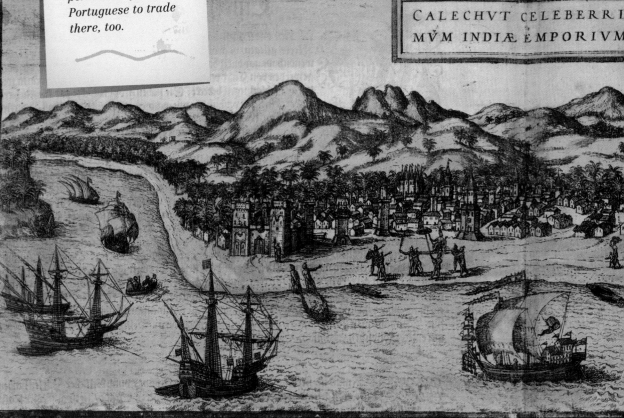

Calicut drew traders from all around the Indian Ocean. Da Gama was given permission for the Portuguese to trade there, too.

CALECHVT CELEBERRI MVM INDIÆ EMPORIVM

DID YOU KNOW?

On the long journey home, so many of da Gama's crew died from disease that he had to abandon one of his ships.

Whether Ibn Madjid personally helped da Gama is not known. In any case, the Portuguese crossed the Indian Ocean.

Landing in India

Da Gama landed in Calicut, India, where he spent three months. He sailed home in August 1498, arriving in Lisbon a year later.

Spices such as pepper, ginger, and cinnamon were very valuable in Europe; they helped disguise the taste of stale or rotten food.

CALICUT

Calicut on India's Malabar Coast was known in the Middle Ages as the "City of Spice." When da Gama arrived in Calicut on May 20, 1498, he found a thriving city. Spices grown on the lush Malabar Coast were brought to Calicut and shipped across the Arab world. Muslim traders controlled the spice trade, which the Portuguese wanted a share of.

1798-1825

NORTH AFRICA

Europeans had been familiar with North Africa from ancient times. The Mediterranean coast had been part of the Roman Empire. But routes further south were blocked by the world's largest desert, the Sahara. In the late 18th century, British and French explorers took more interest in the area. It might provide a route to west Africa.

The German Heinrich Barth explored Lake Chad and the Niger River in the early 1850s. His careful records of everything he found set new standards for exploration.

DID YOU KNOW?

In 1825, Alexander Laing was the first European to reach the fabled city of Timbuktu by crossing the Sahara.

For centuries, the only travelers in the Sahara were Arab and Berber traders. Europeans started to explore there after 1788, when the African Association was founded in London.

A Mysterious River

The first goal was to find out the course of the Niger River. Did it flow east or west? Friedrich Hornemann reached southern Libya in 1798, but failed to find the source of the river. Two Scotsmen, Walter Oudney and Hugh Clapperton, with the English Major Dixon Denham, reached Lake Chad in 1823. It was only the following year that Major Alexander Laing found the approximate source of the river.

DIXON DENHAM

Major Dixon Denham was sent on a British government expedition to set up trade links with west African states. He joined two Scotsmen, Oudney and Clapperton, as they crossed the desert to search for the source of the Niger River in 1821. What they found was Lake Chad. Many people believed the lake was the river's source. Denham showed that the two were not connected.

The Atlas Mountains rise above the rocky Sahara Desert in Morocco. The Sahara included both rocky and sandy desert: both were difficult to cross.

17

THE SAHARA

The Sahara was potentially fatal for Europeans. Temperatures reached 130°F (54°C) in the day but dropped to freezing at night. Sandstorms were frequent. Disease killed numerous explorers. But the mystery of what lay south of the desert kept drawing new explorers.

Sand dunes rise hundreds of feet in the Sahara. They were a formidable barrier to any explorers trying to cross the desert.

The French explorer Henri Duveyrier made close ties with the Tuareg. He lived with them in the desert for a year and wrote a dictionary of their Berber language.

In 1850, the German explorers Heinrich Barth and Adolf Overweg crossed the Sahara on an expedition led by an Englishman, James Richardson. Richardson died on the way, so Barth took command. He and Overweg reached Lake Chad. They carefully mapped the region.

Crossing the Sahara

After Overweg died of disease, Barth carried on alone. He reached Timbuktu. He was joined by another German, Dr. Vogel, but Vogel was killed by native people. Barth returned to London alone nearly six years after setting out.

DID YOU KNOW?

Barth's five-volume account of his travels was one of the most important reference books ever written about Africa.

DESERT NOMADS

For Europeans, it was difficult to imagine anyone surviving in the Sahara. It was too hot, too sandy, and too dry (and too cold at night). But for the Tuareg, the Sahara was home. The Tuareg were nomads, meaning they moved around with their homes. They had learned to adapt to the desert: how to find water, for example, or how to keep cool during the heat of the daytime.

1850–1900

A native canoe is attacked by hippos on Lake Chad in this 19th-century drawing based on the writings of Heinrich Barth.

DID YOU KNOW?

The French planned to build a railroad across the Sahara to reinforce their control of the region. It was never built.

In 1830, the French had invaded Algeria in North Africa. By 1848, Algeria was officially part of France, and the French claimed control of much of the Sahara. Within a decade, French explorers started to head south.

Exploring the Desert

Henri Duveyrier explored the Algerian Sahara in 1860. He lived with the Tuareg for over a year. In 1865, Gerhard Rohlfs, a German working for France, explored Lake Chad and the Niger River. He later explored the edges of the Libyan Sahara. In 1878, however, he gave up an attempt to cross the Sahara eastward, from Lake Chad to the Nile.

The French Take Control

In the 1870s, Gustav Nachtigal spent six years exploring the eastern Sahara, including the Uele River south of Lake Chad. In the early 1880s, Wilhelm Junker showed that the Uele was part of the Congo River system of central Africa. The mapping of North Africa was complete. In 1900, Fernand Foureau led an expedition from Algiers to the Congo. He sealed French control of the entire territory from the Mediterrranean to the Congo basin.

A camel caravan sets out across the Sahara. For centuries, camels have been used for transportation in the world's deserts.

A BEDOUIN CARAVAN

Nomads and traders used long camel caravans to cross the desert. The English explorer Charles Doughty traveled with a caravan in the 1870s. He described how the Bedouin cured the sick with a drink made from donkeys' dung and milk. The caravan was raided by bandits. Doughty called the desert "a wilderness of burning." He became very sick: the hostile climate nearly cost him his life, but eventually he survived.

SOUTH AFRICA

The missionary Robert Moffat preaches in South Africa. He is watched by two local children he and his wife adopted, Sarah Roby and John Mokoteri.

Europeans settled in South Africa in the 17th century. In 1652, the Dutch East India Company set up a base at Cape Town. It was a staging post on the voyage around Africa from Europe to the Indian Ocean. Soon the small colony was booming.

The early Dutch settlers stayed close to the coast, but by 1800, travelers had reached as far north as the Orange River and the edge of the Kalahari Desert.

British Control

During the Napoleonic Wars (1803–1815), the British occupied the cape. Missionaries arrived from Britain, along with naturalists such as William Burchell, who explored inland in search of flora and fauna. The missionary John Campbell traveled the furthest. In 1819, he reached the source of the east-flowing Limpopo River. In 1817, meanwhile, the Scottish missionary Robert Moffat made friendly relations with the Matabele and explored the Orange River system.

THE GREAT TREK

The Boers were descendants from the original Dutch settlers. They disagreed with the British ban on slavery. Between 1836 and 1850, they moved by ox train inland from Cape Town in a migration known as the Great Trek. They settled in two areas: Natal and Transvaal. They clashed with the native Zulu. The Zulu were no match for the Boers' guns; many were killed in violent fighting.

Boers on the Great Trek to Natal had to cross the forbidding Drakensberg Mountains, which the Zulu called the "Barrier of Spears."

1795–1806

MUNGO PARK

Mungo Park was not a typical explorer. When the African Association was looking for someone to find the Niger River in west Africa, it chose a 24-year-old Scottish surgeon who spoke no Arabic. Park was heading into a region where so many explorers had died that it was later called the White Man's Grave.

Mungo Park showed that an explorer in west Africa had to be resourceful, strong, and preferably young enough to stand up to the physical demands.

DID YOU KNOW?

Park arrived in Africa for the first time carrying just a compass, thermometer, sextant, and a couple of pistols.

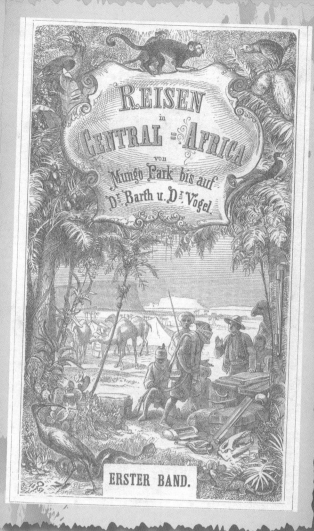

THE NIGER RIVER

The Niger flows 2,600 miles (4,180 km) in a great bend through west Africa, first west to east, then north to south. Its source is in the highlands of Guinea; its mouth is on the Gulf of Guinea in the Atlantic. In the 18th century, Europeans became obsessed with finding out about the mysterious river. The quest drew many explorers, especially after the African Association was formed in 1788 to organize expeditions.

Park headed up the Gambia River and reached the Niger basin in December 1795. He was taken prisoner by the local Muslim ruler, but was eventually released.

The Magnificent Niger

Park reached the Niger in July 1796. He solved one of the great mysteries about the river: it was flowing east. By now, Park was very sick. Friendly natives nursed him back to health. When he returned to Gambia in June 1797, he had been given up for dead.

The final part of the course of the Niger, from Bussa south to the sea, was finally discovered by the brothers Richard and John Lander in 1830.

Park returned to Africa in 1805. This time he was better equipped. He led an expedition from Gambia into the Niger valley. It arrived in the hottest part of the year, just before the rainy season. When the rains came, they brought disease-carrying insects.

Devastated by Disease

Disease and fever wiped out all of Park's pack animals. Two-thirds of the Europeans in his party had died before the expedition reached the Niger River itself in August. By now, Park himself was very sick.

DID YOU KNOW?

The Niger forms a marshy delta at the coast. That made it hard to find a channel to explore the river by sailing upstream.

INSECTS AND DISEASE

Many explorers in Africa died after being bitten by the tsetse fly or the mosquito. The tsetse fly causes sleeping sickness, while mosquito bites spread malaria. Quinine could treat malaria—but many Europeans made the fatal mistake of not taking their medication for long enough, so they died long after they had left Africa.

The survivors sailed hundreds of miles down the Niger. They passed the city of Timbuktu and entered Hausa country. By now, only four men were still alive.

A Mystery

When the boat reached the Bussa rapids, it was attacked by local people. Whether Park and his men were killed or whether they drowned, nobody knows. None survived.

Crocodiles were among the many dangers explorers faced on the rivers of west Africa; others included rapids, hostile natives, and hippopotamuses.

1816–1827

RENÉ CAILLIÉ

René Caillié was the son of a village baker in France. At the age of just 17, he ran away to sea. His voyage took him to west Africa, where he jumped ship. He joined a British expedition looking unsuccessfully for Mungo Park. Then Caillié returned to France for seven years.

This mud-built mosque stands in Timbuktu; the city became a center of Islamic scholarship and was also home to a university.

This 19th-century print shows Caillié and his native bearers crossing a fast-flowing river during the search for Mungo Park.

DID YOU KNOW?

Many people doubted Caillié had seen Timbuktu. His description didn't match the popular images of the fabled town.

Back in Africa in 1827, Caillié heard that the French Geographical Society was offering 10,000 francs for the first man to reach Timbuktu.

Alone to Timbuktu

Caillié disguised himself as a Muslim. He joined Arab caravans at the Guinea coast in March 1827 and traveled with them to Timbuktu. He spent two weeks in the city before returning to Paris to claim the prize.

A LEGENDARY CITY

Many Europeans had heard stories of Timbuktu. It was said to be a city of legendary wealth in the heart of Africa. The city turned out to be rather different from the popular image. Its buildings were all made from mud, for example. But it was indeed wealthy. Lying where the Niger River meets trade routes across the Sahara, Timbuktu had been an important trading center since the Tuareg had founded a settlement there in the 12th century.

1853–1859

BURTON AND SPEKE

By the mid-19th century many of the questions about the Niger River in west Africa had been answered. Europeans came up with a new obsession: the Nile River. No more was known about the river's source than when the ancient Greek geographer Ptolemy had described it in AD 150.

The route upstream on the Nile was blocked by a series of cataracts, where rocks, rapids, and waterfalls made sailing impossible.

Richard Burton's fascination with foreign cultures had already taken him to the Islamic holy city of Mecca in Arabia.

In 1853, the Royal Geographic Society in London decided to send an expedition to east Africa to try and find the river's source. The English adventurer and army officer Richard Burton had already proposed such a trip. He was given the commission. He set off for east Africa with another officer, John Speke.

A Personality Clash

The two men arrived in east Africa early in 1857. They were very different personalities, however. Burton was an intellectual who was fascinated by Arab culture. Speke was mainly interested in hunting game. The pair fell out; their differences later turned to hatred.

TWO NILES

In the early 17th century, Portuguese missionaries reported that the Nile rose in Ethiopia. In 1774, the Scottish explorer James Bruce claimed they were wrong. He had discovered the source further east. His claim caused a storm. In fact, he had found the source of the Nile—but of the Blue Nile, a tributary of the White Nile. As Speke would discover, the Portuguese had been right. The source of the White Nile lay farther south.

Speke was convinced that Lake Victoria was the source of the Nile, not Lake Tanganyika; Speke was proved right.

Burton decided to follow a caravan route with 100 Arab porters. They spent four months reaching Tabora, 500 miles (800 km) inland. Many of the porters deserted; the rest refused to continue. Both Burton and Speke were too sick from malaria to travel on their own.

The River's Source?

Burton, who spoke fluent Arabic, arranged a new caravan. It reached Lake Tanganyika on February 13, 1858. Burton was sure this was the source of the Nile. Speke, however, took a small party to explore an area to the north.

Speke found another lake—Victoria—that he said was a more likely source of the Nile. Burton disagreed. The two men quarrelled. Burton was sick, so Speke returned to England alone.

Taking the Credit

In London, Speke presented his findings to the Royal Geographic Society. When Burton arrived two weeks later, he found that Speke was the hero of the day.

DID YOU KNOW?

Speke named the lake he found after Great Britain's queen, Victoria. It is the largest lake in the world.

A FALLING OUT

Burton and Speke hated each other. Burton was a bad-tempered intellectual, while Speke was an easy-going hunter. Burton never forgave Speke for claiming the discovery of the source on his return to London. The two had agreed that they would present their findings together.

Exploration of east Africa was spurred by the discovery of Mount Kilimanjaro in 1848 and by stories of a series of lakes in the Ethiopian highlands.

SPEKE AND GRANT

In 1860, the Royal Geographical Society sent John Speke back to Lake Victoria to try to prove his theory about the source of the Nile. Speke's companion this time was James Grant. But Speke was forced to leave Grant as a hostage with a local chief in order to be allowed to continue his journey. He went on to the lake alone.

Speke (standing) and Grant failed on their first attempt to reach Lake Victoria because local people were hostile; on the second attempt, Grant was taken hostage by a local chief.

This 19th-century photograph shows Ripon Falls, where the Nile River flows out of the northern end of Lake Victoria in what is now Uganda.

After two years in the bush, Speke arrived in July 1862 at the point where the Nile flowed out of Lake Victoria. He named the place Ripon Falls. He rushed back to rescue Grant. The men traveled to Gondokoro, where they met Samuel Baker and his wife, Florence, who were also looking for the Nile's source.

A Disputed Claim

Grant and Speke returned to London convinced they proved the source of the Nile. But their claim was challenged. First, the Bakers found another lake they said was the source. Second, Speke and Grant could not prove that the river that left Lake Victoria actually flowed into the Nile.

DID YOU KNOW?

"The Nile is settled," read a telegram Speke sent from Khartoum to London—but his old enemy Burton disagreed.

A TRAGIC DEATH

Among those who challenged Speke's discovery was Richard Burton. He said that Speke could not be 100 percent certain that the source was Lake Victoria. He still believed it was Lake Tanganyika. A public meeting was arranged to debate the issue in September 1864. The day before, Speke died from a gunshot wound. Some people thought it was suicide—but it was probably an accident.

SAMUEL AND FLORENCE BAKER

The wealthy Englishman Samuel Baker wanted to find the source of the Nile and to meet Speke and Grant. On a first expedition in 1861–1865, with his wife Florence, he did meet the explorers. He also discovered Lake Albert, which he wrongly thought might be the source of the Nile River.

Baker discovered a spectacular waterfall in Uganda. He named it Murchison Falls, for the president of the Royal Geographical Society in London.

DID YOU KNOW?

Florence Baker could speak fluent Arabic, which she had learned while she was a slave in an Ottoman harem.

In 1869, Baker and Florence returned to the Nile. The khedive, or ruler, of Egypt was a British ally. He hired Baker to help him conquer warring tribes in southern Sudan. Baker sailed up the Nile from Khartoum with the largest-ever expedition in Africa: 58 boats and 1,600 men. He defeated the tribes, but the Khedive soon lost power in the area.

A Failed Mission

Baker wanted to prove that Lake Albert was a source of the Nile. But he was unable to make a breakthrough from the lake to the river. Lake Albert was not as significant as Baker thought. Later explorers would confirm Lake Victoria as the river's source.

FLORENCE BAKER

According to Samuel Baker, he found his second wife in an Ottoman slave market and bought her. Florence was from Transylvania, which was then part of the Ottoman Empire. She spoke many languages, rode camels, and carried a pistol. After sharing Baker's African adventures, she settled in England with him, where she was known as Lady Florence.

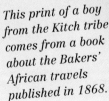

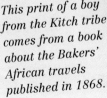

This print of a boy from the Kitch tribe comes from a book about the Bakers' African travels published in 1868.

1849–1873

DAVID LIVINGSTONE

The Scot David Livingstone was the most famous of all African explorers. He was born into a poor family and worked in a cotton mill as a child. But Livingstone later trained as a doctor. He moved to South Africa in 1841. He worked for the famous missionary Robert Moffat.

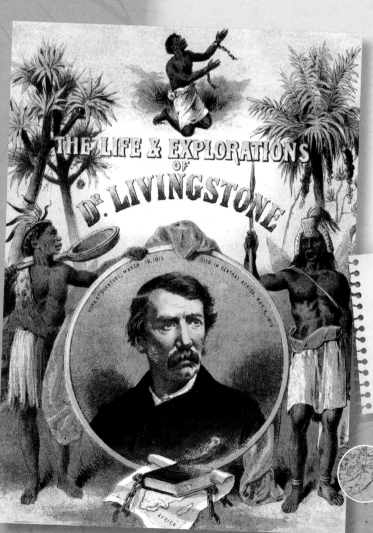

Livingstone was a superstar of the age; people around the world were desperate to read about his adventures in newspapers and books.

DID YOU KNOW?

Livingstone discovered the huge Victoria Falls on the Zambezi. Local people called the falls "the smoke that thunders."

In Africa, Livingstone's quest to find converts led him into becoming an explorer. From 1849, he made several expeditions into central Africa. He visited the Makalolo people on the Zambezi River near Sesheke in 1851.

Coast to Coast

In 1853, Livingstone returned to the Makalolo, and from there, he headed to the west coast at Luanda. He rested because he was sick, then headed back to Sesheke. He reached the Zambezi and pressed on down the river to the coast at Quelimane. He had crossed the continent from west to east. The trip made Livingstone a popular hero.

SIDI BOMBAY

One of the most traveled explorers of Africa was Sidi Mubarak. Born in east Africa, he had become a slave. His Arab master took him to India, which is where he got his nickname. Sidi Bombay acted as a caravan leader and interpreter for explorers such as Burton and Speke. When Livingstone became lost, Sidi Bombay accompanied the expedition to find him.

This illustration shows Livingstone and one of his children at Lake Ngami in 1849; Livingstone's family made many of his trips with him.

Livingstone continued to explore, often using a steamship to follow rivers. His discoveries, such as Lake Nyasa, helped geographers who were trying to understand the shape of Africa.

Hunt for the Nile

In 1866, Livingstone traveled into central Africa to seek the source of the Nile. An opponent of slavery, he had to make alliances with local Arab slave traders. His porters ran away and supplies failed to arrive. At Lake Tanganyika, he fell sick for most of 1870 with fever.

Livingstone made one last effort to find the source of the Nile. He set off in 1871 but failed. He was ambushed by tribesmen and was lucky to escape alive.

A Desperate Situation

Livingstone had no supplies left. He did not know if his messages had reached the outside world. Unknown to him, however, the hunt to save him had already begun.

MARY LIVINGSTONE

The daughter of Livingstone's employer, Robert Moffat, Mary was born in South Africa. She married David in 1844. She and her children often traveled with Livingstone in Africa. Mary was brave and courageous. She died from fever during a trip to Africa's Great Lakes with her husband in April 1862.

Livingstone found the spectacular waterfalls on the Zambezi on November 17, 1855. He named them Victoria Falls, in honor of the British queen.

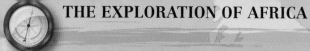

HENRY M. STANLEY

Welshman Henry Morton Stanley went to sea as a boy and jumped ship in the United States. Before his legendary meeting with Dr. Livingstone, he had lived a colorful life. His later exploration was controversial, however. It opened the way for a huge increase in slavery in central Africa.

This print shows the famous meeting at Ujiji between Henry Stanley (left) and David Livingstone in October 1871.

Porters celebrate in this illustration showing Henry Stanley emerging from the jungle in the Belgian Congo at the end of an expedition in 1889.

In October 1869, Stanley was working as a journalist for the *New York Herald*. He received a two-word telegram from his editor, James Bennett Jr.: "Find Livingstone!"

In Livingstone's Footsteps

In early 1871, Stanley led a 200-strong party from Zanzibar to the mainland and toward Lake Tanganyika. At the end of October, he arrived in the village of Ujiji on the side of the lake. On his way, he had crossed a swamp and narrowly avoided a rebellion by the Nyamwezi tribe against their Arab rulers. Livingstone left his hut to meet the white man who he heard had arrived in the village.

FAMOUS GREETING

Stanley's greeting when he met the explorer is famous: "Dr. Livingstone, I presume? I thank God I have been permitted to shake hands with you." "I feel thankful that I am here to welcome you," said Livingstone. Even though they were in the middle of Africa, the two men spoke in the formal way they would have used if they had met in the middle of a Western city.

The two men struck up a friendship. They traveled to the end of Lake Tanganyika. Then Stanley returned to England to report his success. Livingstone continued his quest for the Nile. He traveled to Lake Bangweulu, where he died on May 1, 1873.

East–West Crossing

Stanley decided to return to Africa. In November 1874, he led an expedition inland from the east coast. Eventually he followed the Lualaba River to the Congo River and then all the way to the Atlantic Ocean at Boma. His 999-day trip had taken him across the continent from east to west.

From the Congo, Stanley traveled into the Rift Valley in 1887. He was the first European to see the Ruwenzori Mountains.

DID YOU KNOW?

Stanley treated his porters harshly. He did not care if they died or deserted; he simply hired more to replace them.

Europeans in east Africa often had to cooperate with slave traders, like the Arab trader Tippu Tip, who helped David Livingstone.

King Leopold's Colony

Stanley had not finished his explorations. In 1879, King Leopold of Belgium decided to create his own empire in the Congo. He hired Stanley to set it up. Between 1879 and 1884, Stanley set up trading centers. He treated the native people poorly, putting down rebellions by force.

THE BELGIAN CONGO

The colony that Stanley helped set up in the Congo was not a Belgian colony. It belonged to one man: King Leopold. Leopold was eager to exploit his colony. His officials enslaved the native population. They made them collect rubber. If the workers did not reach their targets, they had their hands or feet cut off. There was an outcry in Europe about such cruelty. Stanley's exploration had been used for a terrible purpose.

GLOSSARY

cape A headland that juts into the ocean.

caravan A large group of pack animals and people traveling together.

colony A settlement founded in a new territory by people from another country.

continent A very large landmass.

expedition A journey made for a particular purpose.

game Animals that are hunted for pleasure rather than for food.

interpreter Someone who translates what someone else is saying into another language.

latitude The position of a location on Earth's surface either north or south relative to the equator.

missionary A person who preaches in order to persuade other people to convert to a religion.

naturalist A scientist who studies or collects plants and animals.

nomad Someone who has no permanent home but who moves around from season to season.

porter A member of an expedition who is paid to carry luggage.

quadrant A device used to measure the angle of heavenly bodies above the horizon.

rapids A part of a river where the current runs quickly over many rocks.

sextant A device used for navigation by measuring the height of the sun or other heavenly bodies.

source The place where a river begins.

tributary A smaller river that runs into a bigger one.

wilderness An unsettled region where nobody lives.

INDEX

FURTHER INFORMATION

Books

Arignello, Lisa. *Henry the Navigator: Prince of Portuguese Exploration*. Crabtree Publishing Company, 2006.

Bodden, Valerie. *To the Heart of Africa* (Great Expeditions). Creative Paperbacks, 2012.

Koestler-Grack, Rachel A., and William H. Goetzmann. *Vasco da Gama and the Sea Route to India* (Explorers of New Lands). Chelsea House Publications, 2006.

Otfinoski, Steven. *David Livingstone: Deep in the Heart of Africa* (Great Explorations). Benchmark Books, 2006.

Young, Serinity. *Richard Francis Burton: Explorer, Scholar, Spy* (Great Explorations). Benchmark Books, 2006.

Websites

http://africanhistory.about.com/od/explorationofafrica/Exploration_of_Africa
About.com biographies of Livingstone and Stanley.

http://www.ucalgary.ca/appliedhistory/tutor/eurvoya/africa.html
Tutorial from the University of Calgary, Canada.

africanhistory.about.com/od/explorer1/a/Explorers-of-Africa.htm
Directory of many explorers of Africa.

www.metmuseum.org/toah/hd/agex/hd_agex.htm
Metropolitan Museum of Art timeline of Portuguese exploration in Africa.